Fallen Away

poems by

Ron. Lavalette

Finishing Line Press
Georgetown, Kentucky

Fallen Away

Copyright © 2018 by Ron. Lavalette
ISBN 978-1-63534-714-2 First Edition
All rights reserved under International and Pan-American Copyright Conventions. No part of this book may be reproduced in any manner whatsoever without written permission from the publisher, except in the case of brief quotations embodied in critical articles and reviews.

ACKNOWLEDGMENTS

The author gratefully acknowledges that earlier versions of several of these poems previously appeared in the following print or online journals or anthologies:

Amygdala (Fernophobia)
Apparatus (False Start)
Deep Water Literary Journal (Eurydice)
The Anthology of New England Writers (Samsara)
The Comstock Review (Fallen Away)
Conspire (Later She Said)
The Country Mouse (Looking In)
The Crescent Moon Journal (Outbound, and Cold Snap)
Greek Fire (Icarus, These Days)
New Works Review (Crossing)
The Orange Room Review (On Tour with The Percussives)
Stirring (The Great Awakening)

Publisher: Leah Maines
Editor: Christen Kincaid
Cover Art: Ron. Lavalette
Author Photo: Ron. Lavalette
Cover Design: Elizabeth Maines McCleavy

Printed in the USA on acid-free paper.
Order online: www.finishinglinepress.com
    also available on amazon.com

Author inquiries and mail orders:
Finishing Line Press
P. O. Box 1626
Georgetown, Kentucky 40324
U. S. A.

Table of Contents

Samsara 1
Fallen Away 2
Crossing 3
Fernophobia 4
Car 5
On Tour With The Percussives 6
Looking In 7
Two I Couldn't 8
Eurydice 9
False Start 10
Later She Said 11
Valentine's Day 12
Seeing Margot 13
Current Events 14
November Looms 15
The Great Awakening 16
Outbound 17
She Goes Away 18
She Goes Away (II) 19
She Goes Away (III) 20
She Goes Away (IV) 21
She Goes Away (V) 22
She Goes Away (VI) 23
Cold Snap 24
Heart 25
Full Punxsutawney Moon 26
Icarus, These Days 27
Still, Though, Beggars Walk 28
Inventory 29

Samsara

Almost 20 years later, I find the Buddha.
I know him instantly. Each of us has aged,
lugging around our bellies, and I, too, am bald.

I see him through the window. Even at night,
six horizons from home, even through a sheet
of glass in sheets of rain, I know him instantly.

I know how the Buddha was broken. I go in
and tell the man how the Buddha was fired
from the dense, oily clay of the Black River,

his cracked glaze an accident of temperature.
I tell the man the Buddha's mostly clay and glue;
tell him that the Buddha, shattered, has fallen

time and again for the same reasons; fallen,
time and again a foolish, foolish Buddha.

Fallen Away

I don't *know* when it happened;
I let it all fall away. I let it fall

on the long drive to work in the morning
in the sunlight, let it fall crossing

ridge after jaded ridge, fall
with the glimpse of an unlikely hawk

or a capture of crows, or the stacking
of cordwood, the season's final frost,

fog on the hillside, or the flutter
of a yellow kite in a midsummer wind.

Like the stones of the dead, untended
in the long grass in the middle of June,

in the middle of nowhere I let it fall,
left it all behind and disappeared,

slipped into seamless dreams, drifted
through blue nights and black mornings.

I watched the water boil for coffee,
sat by the river and watched the water

run away toward heaven, heard angels
whisper in the leaves, left the secret

undiscovered, saw the uncertain moon
swim, reflected in dark, starlit pools.

Gone, now, the last of all the wasted words;
the effort, senseless, of upward struggle.

Crossing

The river sings of its rocks, mirrors
emerald and jade where summer
shadows attempt to outrun
sundown. I intrude, I presume,

I stand near the middle. The second cut
of hay is on the banks, neatly ordered
in rows this time of year, golden,
measuring the march-step toward August.

I think about changes: the movement
of sand through narrow places, how
a ripple diminishes downstream,
how a sound sounds when it stops.

Fernophobia

Nearly dawn
near the border:
Seconal, Valium, booze.
No one expected
the slow opening of eyes,
least of all
the man among the ferns, dismayed.
This was to be the longest sleep,
the rest, at last, so well-deserved.
Imagine his surprise:
dew-soaked, a slug
across the bridge of his nose,
no shoes or recollection.

Car

I'd like to go out now, in a car
with my friend—a stolen car
with a cigarette smell in it, I think,
or the owner's perfume or cologne—
and drive it with the windows down
or let my friend drive; take it down
by the riverbend where the big stones
muscle up to the bank and stars wink
overhead, tiny, silver, deep in the black
night, bluesy, reflected in the black
backwater, the surface still. We'd light
up a smoke, sit on the stones, stoned, dream.
I'd like to go out driving now in the dark air
with my friend at the wheel, breathe the air
down where the rock-filled river screens
the lights of the city, leaves only stars, bright.

On Tour with the Percussives

Every nook held its gong, its cowbell
tabla, tamboura, tom-tom, conga, guiro
and that was all we ever knew
except for how the landscape scrolled
past the tinted windows, lights
in little houses in tiny towns
well before dawn on the fringe
of the city, no one up but us,
not even the paperboys. We'd
hear the rev-down, feel the bus
decelerate, suffer the first tug
of gravity, re-enter atmosphere, peer
out at the still-dark garage,
the unlit pumps waiting, sway
slightly when the brakes squeaked,
unaccustomed as we were
to stationary objects.

This was always the golden moment:
stepping off the bus onto pea-stone,
sunrise still an hour beyond horizon,
all the air in every direction pregnant,
everything only *about* to happen;
we'd share a quiet smoke and
listen to our heartbeats, rehearsing.

Looking In

Fully banqueted,
the nicotine outcast
scavenges cigarettes poolside
while dregs of the party
sip Tanguerays with tonic
and linger over cheesecake.

Nothing is as blue as the pool.
The night, narcotic, welcoming,
lengthens; spreads itself out
behind a buttery August moon.

In the morning, huddled
over coffee, everyone is
blown dry by sunrise
and smells like almonds.

Two I Couldn't

One said it would take some lace
to make the scattered buzzing cluster,
set it migrating toward a center
like bees in a humming hive; would take
some stems and blooms to make her
come and feel alive. Instead,
I read her frozen litanies
of things I could not muster;
sent her only gyrating prose.
She dozed; arose to see a me
she'd never known. This,
I realize, is why I've slept alone.

Another each night shot herself and
urged me to do likewise, or, otherwise
she said she sank like sad Eurydice, doomed
and dead, and rightly forgotten. Hot and
bothered and under the influence, I, a sucker
for a confluence of thighs, drank a glass
of rotgut, but not so fast or often that I lost
my focus; often enough that it broke us
down our middles. We ceased to play and I,
an Orpheus without his fiddle, slunk away
and called her on the phone. I've slept alone;
have seen the long, hard evenings soften.

Eurydice

She goes to that dark land
of her own free will
and far too often.

She blames it on snakebites:
something inside writhes, closes.
Below, something opens
invites her in, insists;
she does not resist.

In the morning, dazed,
apologetic,
she rises, stares
burning in the day's light
she barely sees
then turns again,
descending.

I am no Orpheus
to follow her there.
I let her fall.

False Start

Maybe this is what happens. A man starts
reading a story in the morning:
                                      a woman
leaves, leaving her laundry and saying
goodbye to the neighbors as they load up
a truck, preparing to leave the neighborhood
forever. She goes to the store and overhears
her husband's girlfriend telling the clerk
how they've played her for a fool, how
his promises of fidelity are a joke,
have always been nothing but a joke.
The woman drives home and says goodbye
again to the neighbors. She leaves her
laundry hanging on the line and goes
into the house, packs a hasty bagful
of whatever's close at hand, says a last
goodbye to the neighbors and drives away
deliberately. Her car breaks down. She
pounds the wheel and waits a fuming hour
for her father to come and rescue her.
She sees the taillights backing up
to her bumper, but when she feels
the first tug of the tow chain, she has
her second thoughts.
                            The man has to
stop reading and go to work. All day long
he thinks about the woman, thinks about
the unfinished story and the neighbors,
packing up to leave. At lunch he goes out
and sits by the lake, starts writing a story
about leaving. After only a page he has to
get back to the office. His wife is away
at a conference. He wants her to come home
and read it. Maybe he never finishes the story.

Later She Said

Later she said
when you see her see if
she's got those names right
see if she's got that list
or the numbers reversed or
what was his name on the paper there
The doctor ought to know

See if she thinks
we should save it
if it's red again or
check the list and see if
you can find out if she's
waiting for the doctor
or she knows if I'm
having any pain or not

Tell her it's red again
Tell her to tell the doctor it's red

Valentine's Day

No one goes there now.
For days the smooth snow,
unbroken to the treeline,
lifted there by wind
along the ridge, settles
at last among the stones.
At night, stars, high,
hiss an inaudible static,
dance for the dead.

In the morning,
if there is sun,
what little sun there is
washes down between the stones,
lights but does not warm.
Cold reigns,
and I stand in the drift,
nearly orphaned.

Seeing Margot

Two or three times a month or more
I tell her about being rounded up
for extermination, or running out of pills
in the middle of the night. Sometimes
she waits patiently while I caress my lies
or opt, instead, to spend my time describing
the baby I found frozen on the lawn. Sometimes,
following her upstairs, I think about how I left
Dr. Zimmerman high and dry, owing him
thousands and thousands of dollars
and I remember Trudy back in Brattleboro,
watching me leave and asking if I'd gotten the cure.
Yesterday I let my watch read 11:50 all day long.
Late in the morning, something like snow came
spitting down, overwhelming my wipers.
Crossing Main near midnight, I saw Margot
through the windshield. I wanted to get out
and tell her that I've lived before, tell her
that the exterminators are coming around
to gather us up again, that I need to see her now
for an hour or so, need to have some coffee
need to take my pills, go home,
scrape the baby off the wet grass.

Current Events

Fwim ted de mommiefish,
fwim if oo tan...

but it was too late,
too late. Her many silver
children, sadly unschooled, netted
only death, provided only
one small unsatisfying meal
for the insatiable clattering
leviathan, working its way
along the shallows, swallowing.

Daily the nightly news blared and
all the careless cavefish, distant,
buried their heads in sandbars, blindly
reading only the sports page, the
market report, the alleged comics.

Lured into compliance, lulled
by the infomercials and the
ever-present sitcoms, caught up
in the water over the dam,
everyone went with the flow.
No one was laughing now.

November Looms

Long before there's light,
he sees small patches of snow
glowing in the dark mulch
at the base of rosebushes,
clinging to rhododendrons.

By mid-day, no trace remains;
only the smell of wet soil
and lingering frost. The sun
is bright but sends no heat.
It might as well be only
what it is: feeble and a
hundred million miles away.

A hundred million miles.
He calculates the airfare.

The Great Awakening

Oily America swims in a red sea
while we sleep. In the morning, the news
is grim; is no news, really; is only more
of what we have come to expect:
the buffed and baritone correspondent,
straight faced, numbly earnest
telling us *Jim, the news death tonight death*
from death this death city is
death is all around us and we fear fear
we miss our mothers and everywhere we look
is blood and destruction, Jim,
and that's about the sum of it
from here in deathville;
back to you in the studio. Jim?
and Jim goes right on reading
the market reports and the weather
and the story about the farmer
who raised a gigantic potato
as smart as the President but
kinder and gentler; and all about
the elections and campaigns
all across America to have Jesus
back in the classroom, Christ
returned to Christmas, churches
to be the agency for insuring the poor,
and so on and so forth until, finally,
finally, finally hot young Jessica's tits appear
at halftime, the cheerleaders take the field
and all's right with the world again,
praise the lord.

Outbound

1.

It's hard to find you
gone tonight, outbound

among the stars, and I
wingless, without a song

under a dimelike moon
look up from ice.

2.

I did not dream,
last night, the loose end

would ravel. Your departure
loomed. I held my breath

while you slept, tired,
tried to imagine you

far from these sheets
of snow, under another sky.

She Goes Away

She goes away, enjoys a little
slice of big city pie. He stays
at home with his desk, thinks
green thoughts. On Telfer Hill
everything moves, everything stays
in its place: he sits on grass,
counts on clouds for shade.
It's like the bottom of an
ocean at the top of the world.

She Goes Away (II)

She goes away for a while
and he goes out for Chinese
every night, goes out for a
long ride in the bright green
afternoon, happy at the wheel
of an old red pickup, driving
through June, Wheels of Fire
blasting on the stereo. She
has a drink in the hotel bar
and he catches a rainbow
trout in the morning, thinks
about catching a plane to
be with her, but changes his
mind when the weather changes,
when the heat rises, when the sun
beats down, beating down his
will to see the south. She
calls him every night and he
calls her darling, kisses her
goodnight across the miles
kisses the phone goodnight.

She Goes Away (III)

She goes away for a while, takes
her daughters and her grandsons
and half of her grandsons'
summery vacation and flies away.
She calls him every night, tells him
it's hotter than hell, tells him
about smog and margarita fireworks.
He takes to flying his kite in the
empty living room at three AM,
afraid to sleep, afraid to sleep
alone. In the morning, his first
half pot of coffee tastes like 1942
crankcase oil.

She Goes Away (IV)

She goes away for a while
to a large southern city and
he wakes up in a small motel
room, hungover, in his old
home town. He's been up late
the night before, up late
the night before that; wakes up
after a dream about scorpions
in the mailbox and a small black
snake coiled in the haybales
he left behind, drying. He calls
her but the phone only rings
and rings and no one answers.
He drives by his old house, thinks
about driving by again, but turns
at the corner, heads for home
hoping the phone is ringing.

She Goes Away (V)

She goes away for a while and
he eats ice cream every night
at two in the morning, puts his
coffee cups in the washer like he's
putting babies to sleep, like he's
mailing her a letter, telling her
everything's under control, everything's
fine, fine; saying he's having lunch
every day down by the lake, flying
his kite every morning in the windy
back yard, sitting down at his desk
every night to write to her, telling her
how everything's fine, fine, just fine.

She Goes Away (VI)

She goes away and he moves
through the house like a rattled
ghost, frightening even the dark
corners with his deep sigh, finds
barely enough energy to brew
coffee and wait for the phone.
She calls him to say she's alright
everything's running smoothly
and he tells her that the sheets
are a tangled mess without her,
the goldfinches eat but refuse
to sing, the moon is almost full,
come home now.

Cold Snap

Outside for obligatory photographs:
ubiquitous head-shot, profile,
three-quarter profile, bust.
I stand between the battered, rusty
plow, lost in a stand of spruce
and the house's winter windows,
nearly buried by blizzard. I squint
and I will be squinting forever
standing, frozen by the shutters.

When I see myself, inside, later,
at first only pixels, then paper thin,
I am several hundred pounds of meat
none of it lean, leaning on a cane,
a lame spectacle trapped by
reflex and bifocality, with snow
at the temple of my thinning hair.

Heart

It's not *convenient* now, is it,
having one that breaks, daily;
having one that fails.
When I heard you on the phone
I almost escaped knowing your voice.
Here, the leaves are changing;
out on your flats there is fog
and little or nothing to do,
nothing to be done.

Full Punxsutawney Moon

Three days later, early, certainly
well before sunrise, after the graspers

and flashers have packed up and gone,
after the national news has had its say,

under a staring, starry, cut-glass sky
and a moon shivering its way toward

moonset, the groundhog steps warily out,
its snout in snow a foot or more deep.

Relieved, at last, of the press of local
press and the tyranny of network tourists

he lounges in the full moon's light,
each icy whisker distinct, resplendent,

its shadow a mere matter of fact
on otherwise unbroken snow.

Icarus, These Days

Morning: Icarus pursues a correlation
between a red hawk, gliding,
silent on a far dark horizon
and the first slash of sunrise,
dull fire before the day's flames.
But everything intervenes:
meetings that haven't
happened, that won't happen
until after it's light, until after
it's almost dark again;
the coffee that spills,
the words that don't;
the pills and calls
and all the deadly needy
people, ready to be served,
waiting to be saved.

He's an unwilling Tantalus:
a wing he cannot grasp, an
image of small flame spread out
across a wide and empty air,
lifts him from sleep but leaves him,
breathless and parched, unable
to speak; drops him, speechless,
down among the boulders
of another desperate day.

Still, Though, Beggars Walk

I can't he says really breathe
and hardly stopping adds
I wish I could I wish I
could sleep and not wake up
breathless in the middle
of the bed halfway through
the snoring night like
most men must and I guess

he continues after a second's
thought I suppose as long as
I'm wishing I might wish I was
thicker I might wish I was
thinner and I might as well
wish I was well not half a
decade into my sixth and
halfway past my prime and in

conclusion he says I'd like to
be less prone to dribble pee
on early morning floorboards
on the way to the daybreak
john less likely to crap my pants
if I slip on the stairs or sneeze
less willing and able to believe
that only my shit won't stink

Inventory

well past half my days
nights crowd up

sleepless, evidence strewn
or tacked to walls

dirty mindframes
can't release graphics

more than 50 years now
paper flat inventory

no successful loves
small desire too little

wracked health only
walking every day nowhere

Ron. **Lavalette** is a very widely-published writer living on the Canadian border in Vermont's Northeast Kingdom, land of the fur-bearing lake trout and the bilingual stop sign. After spending several decades as a rug sucker and fish picker, he became a Special Educator and Human Services drone and got serious about writing. His work, both poetry and short prose, has appeared extensively in journals, reviews, and anthologies ranging alphabetically from *Able Muse* and the *Anthology of New England Poets* through the *World Haiku Review* and *Your One Phone Call.*

A reasonable sample of his published work can be viewed at EGGS OVER TOKYO: http://eggsovertokyo.blogspot.com

www.ingramcontent.com/pod-product-compliance
Lightning Source LLC
LaVergne TN
LVHW041511070426
835507LV00012B/1494